Time for Freedom?

Services for older people with

learn_____ties

Goo__p____ice in the aftermath

of l__ng___ay hospital closure

J__ne F___zgerald

Centre for Policy on Ageing | Values Into Action

First published in 1998
by the Centre for Policy on Ageing and Values Into Action

Centre for Policy on Ageing
25-31 Ironmonger Row
London EC1V 3QP
Tel: 0171 253 1787
Fax: 0171 490 4206
Email: cpa@cpa.org.uk

Values Into Action
Oxford House
Derbyshire Street
London E2 6HG
Tel: 0171 729 5436
Fax: 0171 729 7797

British Library Cataloguing in Publication Data
A catalogue record for this book is available from the British Library

ISBN 0904139956

The **Joseph Rowntree Foundation** has supported this project as part of its programme of
research and innovative development projects, which it hopes will be of value to policy
makers and practitioners. The facts presented and views expressed in this report, however,
are those of the authors and not necessarily those of the Foundation.

Throughout this report identifying material such as names and other details have been
omitted or disguised by the use of pseudonyms.

Printed by Henry Ling Ltd at The Dorset Press, Dorchester, Dorset, England
Cover design by Jeremy Austen

This report is dedicated to 'Terry':

The title for this report came from a quote from Terry, one of the research participants. Terry lived in a ward in a hospital that was all but closed. All the buildings surrounding the ward were derelict, the views from the windows were of broken down buildings from which the 'lucky people' had long since moved out. The closure of the ward had been postponed numerous times causing confusion and anguish for the people who lived there. Terry felt that he would never be free because even if he moved out, he felt he was 'old' and would always need care. He felt that independence had eluded him because he had been kept in hospital for so long and he should have had the opportunity to move out many years ago. Terry never had the chance to experience life 'outside', he died on the derelict hospital ward shortly before he was due to move out.

★

Jane Fitzgerald, the author of this report, has worked in the field of learning difficulties for many years, both in residential support and in the community with people who have a learning difficulty and their families. She has also studied law and undertook a thesis on sterilisation without consent of women with learning difficulties. She now works freelance in research and training.

BARN OWLS

Harry spends a lot of time on his artwork at which he is particularly talented;
this is an example of his work. (see page 27)

Contents

Acknowledgements

This project was made possible by the generous support of the Joseph Rowntree Foundation. Particular thanks must go to Alex O'Neil for his personal support and encouragement through some very difficult times.

Thanks are also due to Gillian Dalley of the Centre for Policy on Ageing for her continuing guidance and advice, to Jean Collins of Values Into Action for listening and sharing ideas, and for spending many hours poring over various drafts of the report, and to Carol Walker for her valuable comments. The members of the Advisory Group have been most helpful in their constructive suggestions: Andrew Bright, Andrew Dunning, Maria Luckhurst, Bill Ritchie, Christopher Smith, Peter Gilbert and Ken Simons.

I am grateful to Catherine Bewley, also a member of the Advisory Group, for her comments on the draft and for her continued support for the project from beginning to end. I would like to acknowledge, too, the friendly succour of my colleagues at CPA while working on this report.

But, most importantly, huge thanks go to all the people who took part in the research: the relatives, support staff and service managers who gave up their time, and particularly the people who shared their experiences of what it really means to be an older person with a learning difficulty. I hope they feel I have told their stories as they would want them to be told.

Thank you, all of you.

Jane Fitzgerald
January 1998

Information For Older People With Learning Difficulties

This report is about where you live and who supports you. It is about the good and the not so good things that happen in your lives. We want the people who work for you to read the things in the report and make the service better for you.

Chapter 2 is about where you live. Some of you are still in hospital, but there are other places you can live. There are also ways you can be supported to find the place that is right for you. You can be supported to do as much as possible for yourself.

The next chapter is about what you do with your time. This looks at the different things available for you to do and how your support workers can help you develop your interests. Many of you go to day centres during the day and do not often get to meet new people. We want your support workers to find better things for you to do during the day. Then you can learn new things and meet new people.

Chapter 4 is about your friends and family. Many of you only know people where you live and do not get the chance to meet new people. We want your support workers to help you to meet new people and make new friends. We also want you to have help to speak up for yourself. We found things that can help you have your say, like a computer that uses pictures, words and sounds.

The next chapter is about having choice in what you do and where you live. You have the right to say what you want to do and where you want to live. Some of you are supported to do that. We want all of you to be supported to do that. We want people to listen to you and not make decisions for you.

The last chapter tells the people who run your services that they must find out what you want. They must make sure everybody is able to live an ordinary life. We want all the people who work with you to read this and help you make the changes you want.

1

Introduction

Between 1991 and 1993 Values Into Action (VIA) carried out an extensive programme of research in England into resettlement practice from hospital care and the re-emergence of institutional trends in community services (Collins 1992, 1993, 1994). One of the findings of the project was that, in many places, older people with learning difficulties are being denied ordinary life opportunities because their greater age is perceived to increase their disabilities. However, the fact of chronological ageing does not necessarily mean an individual becomes more dependent. Most older people live in their own homes for all or most of their lives. Only a small minority, and then only in their final years when their need for personal care has grown substantially, move into residential or nursing home care.

To exclude people with learning difficulties from ordinary life on grounds of age, when it is widely acknowledged that all people with learning difficulties whatever the extent of their disabilities can enjoy and benefit from ordinary life opportunities, is highly questionable. Even when moving into residential care becomes appropriate, it is important to recognise that the principles of ordinary life and integrated living are extended to these settings (CPA 1996).

The VIA research generally confirmed that the necessary administrative and financial mechanisms do now exist to enable people to move into the supported community accommodation of their choice. It also found, however, that the scope and powerful potential of those mechanisms were often not being fully exploited, frequently because of widespread ignorance, general confusion and lack of understanding as to what it is possible to achieve.

Another important finding from the VIA research was that there remains a significant number of people with considerable influence over hospital closure and resettlement outcomes. Some of these people continue to oppose the hospital closure programme and do not support the objective of enabling all people with learning difficulties to experience ordinary life opportunities. This research concluded that their opposition often stems from their familiarity with institutional thinking and their lack of understanding of the potential of good quality community care. These aspects will be explored in this report.

The VIA study of the hospital closure and resettlement process revealed that lessons learned in successful resettlement programmes are often not transferred from one area to another and that local, sectarian interests continue to influence heavily the course of hospital retraction. One of the groups of people for whom specialist, segregated provision is often proposed consists of older residents. Many of these have lived in hospital for 30, 40, or even 50 years or longer and they have very real doubts about the wisdom of their now moving into the community. Some resettlement schemes, however, have already demonstrated that it is possible for such people to be supported with great success in the community, in ways which enable them fully to enjoy their remaining years. These points will be explored further during the course of this report.

Hospital residents are heavily dependent on the quality of information and advice given to them by staff, relatives and others. If those people are dubious about community care, or believe that older people generally need a more protective environment, then the residents are likely to be influenced accordingly. Research by Walker et al. (1995) found that staff working with older people with learning difficulties often have a strong belief that older people will be more dependent and less capable of learning new skills, despite lack of evidence to support that supposition. Such preconceived notions are likely to impose restrictions on the range of options and opportunities made available to older people.

It was considered timely by the project team to undertake new research which, by asking older people with learning difficulties themselves, would seek to discover how they see the services they receive and what they would like to happen in the future. To gain as full an account as possible of the types of services older people with learning difficulties want and need, this research included people living in a whole variety of different situations ranging from the institution to their own home, as well as people from their social and support networks.

The project was funded by the Joseph Rowntree Foundation and co-ordinated by Values into Action and the Centre for Policy on Ageing.

It is important to note at this stage that this report was not intended as a critique of services per se. It was intended to highlight and promote examples of good practice in services for older people with learning difficulties, hence, the outcomes may be more positive than other research in the field has found. Also, the focus was on services for older people with learning difficulties and not a comparison between services for older people and those for younger people.

The aim of this research is to facilitate the development of appropriate and relevant services for older people with learning difficulties by identifying and promoting good practice examples in terms of:

- meeting people's needs in the way they want them met;
- preparing people for change in positive and sympathetic ways;
- achieving good quality life styles in accordance with the ordinary life principle;
- achieving good integration within the community.

Methodology

The research was carried out in five fieldwork areas across the country, chosen to represent a wide cross-section of geographic, environmental, cultural, organisational and other factors. Detailed interviews were carried out with thirty-one users of services, their carers and service providers. Additional information was obtained through documentation on policies and procedures, as well as by observation of activities and practice in the fieldwork sites.

The study focused on three main categories of people with learning difficulties:

- older people still living in mental handicap hospital;
- older people living in residential homes, group homes or other supported living situations in the community, including older persons' homes;
- older people still living in the family home with very elderly parents, or with other family members.

Interviews were semi-structured to enable participants to pursue topics of particular interest to them, while at the same time shaping and guiding the direction of the interview. Discussion with people with learning difficulties centred on their personal views and choices, including their views on their current support, the kind of services they would like, how they felt about getting old, and what they thought increasing age would, or should, mean for them.

Interviews with their friends, advocates and relatives focused particularly on the twin issues of their views of the support currently being provided, and what kind of service they would like to be provided. Topics pursued with service workers, managers and purchasers included the extent to which they have thought specifically about services for older people with learning difficulties, what impact this has had on practice (if any), and what current thinking is behind plans (or absence of plans) for future provision for this client group.

The ages of the thirty-one people who participated ranged from their late fifties to late eighties. Fourteen of the participants were male, seventeen were female. Two of them lived in hospital and expressed no hope of moving out; seven people lived in hospital though had plans for resettlement; nine people lived in small group homes run either by a housing association or NHS Trust; one person lived in an NHS Trust large community home; three people lived in a large home run by a housing association; one person lived in a supported living network; two people lived in adult placement; two people lived in sheltered accommodation; one person lived in a residential care home; two people lived with relatives; and one person lived in her own home (see Appendix 1).

The aim was to find out the views of the individuals on issues which affect their everyday lives. How involved are they in the decision-making process and what have changes in policy meant to them personally? As has been stated, people who have lived a 'sheltered' or 'protected' life within an institution or been cared for by others, without having the opportunity to learn more about the alternatives, will tend to express the views of those closest to them. Hence we wanted to find out how much the individual had to do with the decisions that were taken regarding their own lives. It became evident during the fieldwork that we would not be able to include the views of many relatives as very few of the participants knew of, or had contact with, their relatives.

Setting the Scene

To understand this report it is important to look at the key issues which affect the lives of older people with learning difficulties and older people in general:

- how are the services funded and managed?
- have there been specific policies developed for older people with learning difficulties?
- financial issues at a national, organisational and personal level

4

- citizenship: for people with and without learning difficulties, ageing is both a personal and a social process.

At a personal level, there are the physical, emotional and psychological experiences of growing older. Different people will have different experiences and responses to this personal process.

Ageing is also a social process that is closely connected with the legal and social aspects of citizenship. For older people who do not have a learning difficulty, where once their status in society (and perhaps also partly their self identity) was based particularly on employment and family roles, status becomes increasingly based on chronological age itself. Though this is not to say that employment and family are no longer part of people's experience as citizens. Employment has a major long-term impact, by dictating the financial circumstances of older people in retirement. For example, many older women are excluded from full participation in society because they do not have the same level of financial resources and independence as older men (Arber and Ginn 1995).

On the one hand, although some family and caring roles may reduce with older age, others may increase. Older people may have new roles as grandparents and carers. On the other hand, Arber and Ginn suggest that women, in particular, may experience ageing as a liberation from family responsibilities and the beginning of new life opportunities. Older people as a group may also develop a new status, for instance as consumers, but this gain depends on financial independence and so will not deliver equal status to all older people.

Citizenship is both a social and legal concept. It is about belonging to, and participating in, society. If citizenship is defined as "participation in the public sphere" (Arber and Ginn 1995), then the social process of ageing tends for most people to reduce the status of their participation in the public sphere. Once people have passed a certain chronological age, they find very real differences in their civil rights. For example, some welfare benefits are not available to people over a certain age, but they become entitled to others by virtue of age; and women over 64 are not automatically included in the national breast screening programme. So, if older people's status around employment and family changes, so do their civil rights and opportunities for involvement in social processes. There is also differential access to citizenship in terms of gender, class, poverty and ethnicity (Arber and Ginn 1995), as noted above.

Changes in the scope of citizenship are often based on society's definitions of 'old age' and assumptions about the biology of chronological age, regardless of individual experience or circumstance. These definitions and assumptions are applied to all people over a certain age (or with perceived characteristics of old age, such as grey hair and a decrease in mobility). So the mass of people, who were just 'adults' differentiated by society in various ways, find themselves grouped together primarily in the category of 'old' and often discriminated against based on membership of this group. Midwinter (1992) calls this "postadulthood, a conception of old age as a stage beyond adulthood, a return to the position of childlike subordination - older people are not included in the category of adults". This difference is enshrined in service organisations: often social services departments are divided into children, adults and older persons teams.

This discrimination, called ageism, is based on a perceived biological category (old age) and a biological process (ageing), acted upon by institutions and held as beliefs by individuals. These beliefs lead to fear and denigration of people with the label 'old', and result in stereotypes about their competence and need for care. This then legitimises the reduction of resources and opportunities to 'old people' as a group (Bytheway 1995). There are similarities between the labelling, and its consequences, of older people and people with learning difficulties, but older people *with* learning difficulties will experience discrimination from both labels.

Ageism, in this way, operates at a societal level but, as noted above, the personal experience of ageing is not necessarily a negative one for individual people. Passing the chronological barrier of 55/60/65 (social, cultural and legal boundaries of 'old' vary) can open new opportunities for personal development and new social roles. Gerontologists have debated for many years whether, how and why older people are excluded from society. The resulting theories (disengagement theory, role theory and so on) often present old age as a negative experience. But older people may also have positive experiences of older age: a liberation from the pressures of younger life; more self-confidence; more time for the self; a chance to review life; new challenges and opportunities.

Many of these issues of citizenship apply equally to older people with learning difficulties. However, older people with learning difficulties are likely to have experienced this exclusion from full participation in society and opportunity all their lives. Their crossing of the chronological boundary into 'old age' may therefore be experienced differently. Individuals will still have a personal response to physical changes of their ageing. There will be personal, social changes as well, as family and friends die and employment and social opportunities, such as they are, change. The opportunities for increased citizenship offered to younger people with learning difficulties may be denied those who are older, simply on the grounds of age. This is ageist and service policies which purport to challenge ageism must therefore also apply their rhetoric and policies to older people with learning difficulties. Older people with learning difficulties should have the opportunity to experience the *benefits* of ageing which those without learning difficulties have.

Historical Perspective

The main push to resettle people from institutional to community care began in the 1970s. The large institutions were to be replaced by small, ordinary homes within the community. The NHS and Community Care Act 1990 placed responsibility for this in the hands of the social service departments with funding to come from both the NHS and local authorities. The resettlement process would be led by social service departments, and people would be resettled into their own locality with the appropriate resources to meet their needs.

How effective has this policy been? There are still institutions for people with learning difficulties which do not have any strategies for closure or policies for retraction at all. This national policy is being implemented in some areas of the country far more expeditiously than in others, so that there are still many people in institutional care, and many of them are older people whom some service providers feel are better cared for within the institution and should therefore remain where they are. A cohesive strategy for the resettlement of all people from within institutional care remains elusive.

Some older people with learning difficulties moved out of institutional care long ago. Some may never have lived in any formal care environment. Unfortunately, many are still waiting for the opportunity to experience life outside the institution. Older people with learning difficulties therefore have a variety of life stories and experiences which will be explored further in this report. Policy and practice development needs to take this into account.

The Report

The report is organised into the following chapters:

Where people live: the environment, who provides support, and whom they live with. Contrasts will be explored between the views of the service users and service providers. Within this, relevant policy issues will be linked as points are discussed.

What people do with their time: occupationally and recreationally. Whether this is meaningful, valued and appropriate according to the individual's needs and wishes. Issues relating to the links between generic and specialist services will be explored along with relevant policy issues. The segregated nature of much of the recreational and occupational facilities will also be explored, how much people are actually integrated into their own communities and how meaningful links are created.

Networks: issues around how people who are segregated from the community are able to forge and maintain meaningful links with people from the wider population. This will include the role of advocates and voluntary schemes such as community service volunteers. How much of an impact do these relationships have on the lives of older people with learning difficulties and what could be done to enable better integration and broaden the horizons of people? This will link into a theme which runs throughout the report but is discussed more in depth in the following chapter.

Choice and Control: this will look at how much of the essence of the individual is lost through block treatment practices and the sheer size of the organisations within which people live. How this can be overcome or minimised with imagination and looking beyond the obvious. Risk-taking and encouraging people to gain confidence and take an active part in the decision-making process which affects all of our lives. Foresight and imagination can create the climate for people to take more control of their lives, from everyday things such as what to wear or eat, to life-changing decisions such as where to live and with whom.

The theme of choice and control is a common thread throughout the report. Choice and control concerns how much each individual has a stake in what is happening in their own lives, how much influence their wishes and desires have on their future plans. Respect and dignity can only come with an element of control over one's own destiny.

8

Organisational protocol and operational strategies: who makes the decisions that will affect people's lives. What policies are in operation within the organisations to provide for older people with learning difficulties. How do these compare with what is happening nationally in provision for older people generally in terms of day and residential facilities? How are the processes of resettlement and provision of services generally affected by the culture of the individual organisations? How can organisations work towards a needs-led, person-centred service and away from the traditional service-centred approach?

Conclusions: this section will bring together the findings of the report. It will discuss aspects of good practice for individuals and how these practices evolved in the organisations studied.

Overview of Research

Service provision for older people with learning difficulties has been an area of growing interest for research over recent years. There are currently a number of projects being undertaken into the different aspects of service provision and delivery to older people with learning difficulties (see, for example, Walker et al. 1996a, SSI 1997). However, apart from the work of Walker et al., there is little written from the perspective of the people themselves, how they feel about the services they receive and what they would like to see in the future. One of the aims of this piece of work is to go some way towards rectifying this.

There is an extensive literature on ageing and old age. Since 1947, the Centre for Policy on Ageing has taken a lead in undertaking research and producing information in the wide field of social gerontology, including service provision, exploring the ageing process and drawing attention to the experiences, both good and bad, of older people as they move through the life course. Research into life transitions and the process of ageing for people in general may have some transferable uses as will be seen through the course of this report, but the crossover rarely happens. One of the aims of this piece of work is to consider the relationship between services for older people in general and services for older people with learning difficulties.

There are prominent researchers in both fields - learning difficulties and social gerontology - whose writings could well be transferable. The work of Alison Norman for the Centre for Policy on Ageing on stereotypes and the negation of the worth of the elderly person is research which applies equally to all older people faced with the discriminatory practices of a society which has little time or focus for older people (Norman 1987). The work of Marian Lewis (1993) on dignity and respect in residential care homes for older people could have been written about many residential care facilities for people with learning difficulties. Loss of choice and control which in turns leads to a loss of identity for people who have to enter residential care is another crossover issue which is thoughtfully discussed by Trevor Blewett (1980) (see also Wynn-Jones 1994, Stocker et al. 1995, Edgerton 1989).

The literature supports the view that caring for people en masse tends to create environments which are not conducive to individuals retaining a sense of dignity and self-identity. The codes of good practice, *Home Life* and *A Better Home Life*, published by the Centre for Policy on Ageing (CPA 1984, 1996) stress the importance of maintaining and promoting individual autonomy in the residential setting as the key to ensuring respect for the dignity of all residents.

The need for providers to look to individual need rather than the label attached to a person, be it 'older person' or 'older person with a learning difficulty' is eloquently described in many works. Walker et al. (1993, 1995, 1996) have done a considerable amount of research outlining the need for an equitable, individual approach to care for older people with learning difficulties.

The development and maintenance of meaningful networks and positive interactions through recreation and occupation are subjects which have also been considered in recent research (Grant et al. 1995, Godlove et al. 1982, Hogg et al. 1989, Lewis 1993). The research tends to conclude that one of the largest deficits of experience for people who live in 'protected' housing is that of personal relationships.

Throughout the report references will be made where relevant to these and other pieces of work. A list of references and further reading appear at the end of this report.

2

Where People Live

"Geographical relocation into local communities, while essential, is not sufficient to ensure that a hitherto devalued and stigmatised group become members of that community." (Walker et al. 1996b)

This chapter looks at the different types of accommodation within which the thirty-one participants of the research live.

NHS Trust Hospitals

Nine of the research participants live in three different hospitals, two of which come under the same management remit: Seal and Heyton hospitals.

Seal Hospital and Heyton Hospital

Seal hospital is all but closed except for a ward on which two of the people who participated in the research, Terry and Edward, still live. The rest of the hospital site has closed down all around this ward and the view for these people is one of derelict, dilapidated relics of the past. At the time the research was carried out, there were ten people living on this ward. They share a dormitory at one end of the ward, and have little or nothing to do at all during the day. There has been some dissent amongst the workforce about the closure which was described by a senior member of staff as *a subtle sabotage of resettlement*. At the time the research was carried out, there was still not a firm closure date despite the ward's dilapidated condition. There was a great deal of uncertainty about when the ward would close and even greater uncertainty about where the people would go. Edward, who was due to be resettled from this ward, did not seem to know much about what was happening at all. He knew it was closing and that he was moving on but was not sure when:

"Not this week is it?" (Edward, 81 years old)

Terry, who is 67 years old, is also unsure of where he is going. He does not want to leave and has not been impressed by the places he has been taken to see:

"They're trying to put me in another home now... I've been there... all you get is your bed, your chair and table, and a toilet to relieve your mind."

Wilfred and Philip, who took part in the research, are located in Heyton hospital. They live on a ward which has no closure date, nor does the hospital. Philip, who is now 84 years old, served his country in World War II. He won medals for his bravery which have since been lost within the hospital. The hospital is separated into large ward units or 'villas'. There are nineteen men living on this ward, all of whom are over 60 years old. The dormitory has been organised into separate living areas for one or two people, although this does not necessarily give the men much more personal space:

"I don't have anywhere to lock anything away... whatever I have gets stolen anyway." (Philip)

The hospital, like many large institutions, was built some distance away from any local services and so the people who live there have everything on site, such as day facilities and medical care for example. Going into the local community is something Wilfred and Philip do on a rotational basis, between all of the people who live on the ward, and is dependent on staff time:

"I go to the community sometimes." (Wilfred, 77 years old)

Even where resources were not a constraint in improving the environment and quality of life, it seemed the ward was still seen as primarily a workplace for the staff:

"All these improvements boost the morale of both staff and residents...everyone likes to work in a pleasant environment and (ward) staff are truly appreciative of their new look home." (taken from a newsletter written by the ward manager)

As there are no plans to close the hospital, neither of these men has any personal resettlement plans in place. The option of resettlement is rarely discussed unless it is instigated by the person themselves:

"If a resident wants to talk about it, we will support a resident." (ward key worker)

From speaking with the two people on the ward, it became clear that they had little knowledge of alternatives to where they were now and Philip, in particular, was quite unsure as to where he would go should he move out:

"Nobody has ever asked me, I don't want to go to another hospital."

Whales Hospital

This is a very large hospital though it is now much reduced in size as there is an active resettlement and closure plan in effect. All of the people living in the hospital are due to be resettled by 1998. The hospital will then close except for the retention of some forensic services on site. Again this hospital has many facilities on site for the people who live there, though there is greater use of mobility cars. From talking to the research participants, going out shopping, or to dinner is evidently more commonplace for the people who live here despite its relative distance from the town. All of the five people interviewed who live in the hospital - Arthur, Winnie, Anne, Emily and Violet - have active resettlement plans in progress. Each of them has an estimated time when they will move on and each of them has been involved in the decision as to where they will go and with whom. Arthur has lived in the hospital for most of his life. He is not able to see and currently lives in a ward with other men which he feels is *"too noisy"*. He is looking forward to moving out; for him it can't come soon enough:

"I've been shown where I will be living to see if I like it, I told the lady to put me there for good then and I won't come back." (Arthur, aged in his seventies)

All of the people who took part in the research at this hospital have had the choice of either returning to where they originally came from, or staying within the area which has been their home for many years. Arthur has a partner in the hospital who comes from a different area. They both want to return to where they came from though the option remains open for them to change their minds if they so wish in the meantime. It is difficult to find the correct terminology to define the relationship between Arthur and Winnie. To use boyfriend/girlfriend is inappropriate when talking of people in their seventies. They do not live together, are not engaged, yet their relationship is intimate and they perceive themselves as being a couple. This report will refer to people in intimate relationships as partners.

13

Two of the women live on the same ward. There are seven people in total on their ward at the moment. There is evidence of a more flexible regime here than at the other hospital. For example, if the evening meal does not appeal to the people living there then the staff endeavour to make something different if they can. The people living here have access to the kitchen to make a drink if they wish, whereas for Philip and Wilfred, this was never an option. Both of these two women know where they will be moving to, though one of them, Anne, who is 81 years old, feels that when she does move out, she would like to have more independence:

> *"I would rather live on my own than live with the people on here... I wouldn't want anyone to look after me I can do it for myself... I could learn to cook."*
> (Anne)

Winnie, the lady who lives on the same ward as Anne, is Arthur's partner. She wants to be with him though she also wants to go back to her family. The choice is ultimately hers. Winnie originally lived in the sister hospital to the one she is living in now; when that one closed, she moved over to this one. She doesn't like to talk much about her time in the other hospital. She is looking forward to moving out and being nearer to her family:

> *"When I go out I want to pay for the electric, water, rent. Buy two beds one for me and one for Arthur...I don't want anyone else, I'll cook for us...I want to move away from here and take Arthur with me."* (Winnie, aged in her seventies)

She says of the two hospitals where she has lived:

> *"Both of them are like prisons, but here at least they only lock you up at night."*
> (Winnie)

The final two women interviewed at Whales hospital, Emily, who is 70 years old, and Violet, who is 86 years old, also live on the same ward, though Violet was convalescing in the hospital block after surgery at a local hospital. The use of the hospital ward is currently under review due to the declining numbers of people living on site and the fact that it does not meet with principles of ordinary living to have a hospital ward on site; *"I think after we lose a few more people there won't really be an excuse for keeping it"* (service manager). Both of these women are fully aware of the fact that the hospital is closing and have been involved in deciding where to

14

go. The ward manager feels that resettlement for older people is inappropriate and that older people should be left where they are, and not have to undergo such a major life change:

> *"Resettlement should concentrate on younger people, to give them their freedom. Older people suffer from transitional shock and often die after being resettled."* (ward manager)

There is no research evidence, however, to support the idea that resettlement leads to early death. One study, for example, found that:

> "In general, studies of de-institutionalisation among people with mental handicap have not shown consequent increases in mortality." (Heller 1985)

NHS Trust Large Community Home

One of the research participants, Gwen, lives in an NHS Trust large community home. All of the people living here will be resettled over the next couple of years and the home will be closed down. There are sixteen people living in the unit, all of them apart from Gwen are in their thirties. Gwen is in her sixties. Gwen uses a wheelchair and lives in a downstairs room which is large enough for her to get around in and has a window at a level that she can see through. This had not been the case previously. Gwen has an advocate/friend, Paul, who has taken time to get to know her very well. He has instigated a multi-media profile which has enabled Gwen to have a pictorial history of who she is. Gwen herself has been totally involved in producing this with Paul and his team. This is a particularly effective system for recording the life history of an individual which is far more personal and has far more meaning to the individual than traditional case notes ever could have.

In Gwen's previous room, Paul had seen that she did not have enough space to move around in her wheelchair. She could not reach the shelves and the window was too high for her to look out. He approached the staff team to discuss a move for Gwen to a room which was not in use. There was much dissent amongst the workforce who felt that the room should be used for other purposes (despite the fact that it had lain empty for some time). It was eventually agreed that she would be able to move in. With the use of the multi-media materials which had been developed, Gwen was actively enabled to participate in how she wanted the room to be arranged and to see a pictorial image of how it would be via a computer.

Gwen will move on from this unit and plans are being developed. The strategic plan involves the people currently living there moving into flats: four people in each flat with three of the flats in one house, though run separately. A plan under discussion for Gwen is that she will move into a two-bedroomed flat. However, the locality within which this unit falls is now being managed by a person who feels that these flats will not necessarily be appropriate and the plan is under review:

The manager's view on living in the community is that: *"It is a right not a luxury to live in the community,"* she went on to say:

> *"There will be full care management and community care assessments at (this unit) and if we decide that people need different placements and the planned flats don't get filled, then so be it."* (service manager)

Housing Association Large Home

Three of the research participants, Maureen, Maude and Margery, live in a large home run by a housing association. They previously lived on a ward in the hospital where Edward and Terry still live. There are nineteen women living here, all of whom are over the age of 60. The unit is located in a semi-rural area which makes community participation quite difficult for the women who live there. However, the women who participated in the research go out on a regular basis to day services, to collect benefits, to the hairdressers and so on. Although there are quite a large number of people living there, the regime is fairly flexible. Breakfast is from the time the first woman gets up until just before lunchtime if someone wants to lie in bed. One of the women, Maude, who is 80 years old, has a room of her own for the first time in her life. She has a key for it but she prefers not to lock it:

> *"I have a key for my room here but I don't lock it. I don't want to but I do have the key."* (Maude)

She is particularly happy living there:

> *"I want to stop here now, what can I say...the staff are very kind, they will do anything for you."*

Having lived in a particularly harsh environment for most of her life (about which she has many stories to tell), this is very important to her.

The other two women, Maureen, who is 84 years old, and Margery, who is 79 years old, share a room at their own request. They both spend a great deal of time in there, watching the television, knitting, or just enjoying one another's company. Maureen has a sister who also used to live in the hospital but was discharged many years ago. It upsets Maureen a great deal when she talks about the hospital, particularly about the fact that her sister was able to leave while she had to stay. She does not know why this happened.

Margery spends mornings in the kitchen helping to prepare lunch. The kitchen is up a flight of stairs which makes it inaccessible to many of the people who live there. There is little that can be done about that due to the nature of the building. However, there is a room with facilities for making drinks which is a little more accessible though it is still down a couple of steps. The women can make drinks whenever they like, for themselves or for others who cannot get down to the room.

Each of the women has a life history book containing photographs and some detail of the hospital where they came from. There was a planned resettlement programme for the women, which included sessions where they could discuss with the resettlement team how they felt about what was happening. For Edward and Terry, who are leaving the same hospital, this has not been the case.

Housing Association Small Group Homes

Eight of the research participants live in small group homes run by housing associations:

- **Calder Association:** Jim who is 66 years old and Don who is also in his sixties, live in the same house. They share with two other younger people;

- **Allons Association:** Theresa who is 58 years old and Tom who is 56 years old, live in the same house. They share with three other people of mixed ages;

- **Kielder Association:** Harry who is 61 years old, lives in a group home with six other people who are younger than he is;

- **Brant Association:** Mabel who is 62 years old, lives in a house which is part of a core and cluster network of housing run by the social services

17

department. The core of the system is the main house which provides a central focus for the service, the cluster or satellite houses, are linked to the core house for support. Mabel lives with one other person.

- **Buttermere Association:** John and Lily who are both in their seventies, live in different group homes run by the same housing association. They each live with five other people;

The houses operated by the first four associations listed are run on similar principles, which are to enable each person to maintain and further develop their independence. There are minimal staffing levels at all times. The people who live there are encouraged to develop networks and links outside the house and to care for their own needs. Meals are cooked by each individual, either just for themselves or on a rota basis for the rest of the people living there. Each of the houses was within easy reach of local facilities or was well served by public transport. There have been some difficulties. Jim (Calder association) recently had to undergo surgery and now requires more assistance than the house would normally be required to give. This has been maintained by using the primary care team and by using extra care workers for specific tasks. However, the long-term situation for Jim is unclear and will be discussed further in Chapter 6, as will the situation regarding registration of group homes which can cause difficulties in terms of the age range of people who are able to live in the houses and in terms of the resources they can offer.

Tom (Allons association) would like to live in a bungalow with his partner:

> *"I've got my name on the list for a bungalow* (the manager of his present house) *helped me do all that, I'm just waiting now."*

John and Lily live in two different houses run by the Buttermere association. There appears to be some differences of opinion amongst the workers within the organisation as to how the house management should deal with the potential need for increased resources as the tenants grow older.

The manager of the home where John lives stated:

> *"As people get more frail and in need of greater physical care, its going to be impossible to keep them 'forever'. Some are going to need nursing home care quite soon...we wouldn't expect to have nurses coming into our home every day - at that stage we accept having to move into a nursing home and so it will be with John."* (home manager)

A staff member at the home where Lily lives, which is run by the same organisation, stated:

> *"Why should Lily move out if she needs more care? This is her home. We would expect outside help to be bought into our home."* (care worker)

NHS Trust Small Community Home

One of the research participants, Henry, who is 61 years old, lives in a house which is run by the local NHS Trust. However, this situation was due to change shortly after the research was completed as the houses were to be taken over by a housing association. The situation for Henry was similar to that of the people living in the housing association group homes. There was minimal staffing though extra provision was made for a man who lives there who has Alzheimer's disease. The homes manager felt it appropriate to enable this man to remain in the environment he knows well and with the people whom he knows and know him: *"Where we do have people who require additional support over and above what we have been funded or required to give, we have put it in"* (homes manager).

Henry goes to the local adult training centre four days a week and stays at home one day a week to take care of his cleaning and other domestic chores and to go out if he so wishes. The house is located reasonably near to the town centre facilities though Henry does not go out on his own. He has some mobility and hearing difficulties. He has his own bedroom on the ground floor of the house and lives with two other people.

Housing Network Scheme

One of the research participants, Doris, who is 59 years old, lives in a supported living network. She lives on her own but is part of a network of others who are all supported by an independent living team. Doris was not sure about the network. She didn't seem to know much about the service providers and she appeared to be quite lonely and isolated.

Adult Placement Scheme

Two of the research participants live in two different adult placement schemes. The principle of adult placement is that a person is given the opportunity to live within an ordinary family home as a member of the family.

- Connie, who is 64 years old, lives with two other women in the home of her carer, her carer's husband and their teenage son. The women live in an annexe to the house which is accessed via the main house. They have their meals in the main house but tend to spend most of the rest of their time in their own rooms. They have a separate living room and their own bedrooms along with a small kitchenette, although they do not make any drinks for themselves as their carer does everything for them:

  "I do mostly everything for Connie, like washing and ironing, cooking and cleaning, simply because I wouldn't trust her to do things, she's so clumsy she would fall over and hurt herself." (adult placement carer)

- Joseph, who is 60 years old, lives with his partner in a flat at the back of their carer's house. Again, they spend much of their time in their flat, coming into the main house for meals and for use of the bathroom. They are not able to make drinks for themselves in their own flat though Joseph would very much like to.

  "We sit in her kitchen there to have our food, she does all the washing, cooking and cleaning." (Joseph)

Residential Home For Older People

One of the research participants, Bob, who is in his seventies, lives in a residential home for older people. There are thirty-eight people living there in total. The use of large residential homes for older people with learning difficulties will be discussed further in Chapter 6. Bob does little for himself here. There is one other older person with a learning difficulty living within the home and according to the manager *"(they) tend to be looked after by the others, they don't cause any problems"*.

However, it would appear that there is some conflict within the service regarding Bob and the other older person with a learning difficulty living in the home:

> *"These people can sometimes be awkward and irritating for the normal residents to put up with."* (manager)

Sheltered Housing/Warden Control

Two of the research participants live in this form of accommodation:

- Dorothy, who is 59 years old lives in sheltered housing. Dorothy has her own self-contained flat but there are also communal rooms where she meets the others for tea and a chat when she wants to. There is warden assistance when needed.

- Fred, who is 68 years old, lives alone in a warden-controlled bungalow which is within walking distance of the village. Fred cares for himself on a day-to-day basis and the warden comes in every morning to see him and he also gets further assistance once a week to enable him to manage his affairs. He has two cats from whom he gets great pleasure. He is also very friendly with his neighbour and they help each other out from time-to-time. Fred used to live in the local hospital for people with learning difficulties. He moved out to live with two other men, was offered the bungalow and accepted. He has managed extremely well since he moved into his bungalow. He does all his own shopping and cooking: *"It's no problem as I've got a fridge and a freezer."*

Relatives

Two of the research participants live with relatives:

- Frank, who is 57 years old, lives in his parental home. Frank lived with his parents until they died He now remains in the family home though totally supported by his sisters who take it in turns to be in the house with him and take care of him. They started the regime of caring when their mother was ill and just carried on after her death, looking after Frank in the same way. Frank does little for himself as his sisters do it all for him:

"There is no need for Frank to go shopping because (his other sister) *gets everything they need on the way here. Her husband brings her in the car and they stop on the way. Its easy, and she knows what Frank wants."* (Frank's sister)

Frank's sisters never take him anywhere because they are so busy just looking after him; any spare time they have is spent with their own families. They are so busy maintaining the same regime within which Frank lived with his parents (which is one of totally 'looking after' all of Frank's needs for him such as cooking, cleaning and generally maintaining the house) that they do not feel they have the time to consider developing it or building on it. They do not include Frank in family activities.

Since the death of their mother they have accepted the social services offer of short-term care for Frank and he now goes to a small residential home for the weekend every two or three months. They accept that Frank likes going *"because they take him out - they go places"* (his sister's words).

- Valerie, who is 68 years old, lives with her brother who is now 72 years old. She lived with her parents until they died and then moved in with her brother and sister-in-law who has since died. Her brother could not bear the thought of having Valerie *"put away"* so has taken on the caring himself. Valerie goes to a residential facility for short-term care every five weeks or so. Her brother worries about what will happen to Valerie if, and when, he is no longer able to look after her. He knows she will probably move into a small care home locally, but he still regards that as *"putting her away"* and feels that she will miss her own home.

Own Home

One of the research participants, Eve, who is 75 years old, owns her own home. Eve lived for many years with her family. She married a soldier who died during World War II. Since that time she has lived in different institutions, the final one being the one where Arthur and the others remain. Eve moved out initially around fifteen years ago into a housing association property with another woman. She wanted to move out of the house and so different possibilities were explored with her as to where she could go. As Eve had lived in a housing association property, she had accrued a discount should she wish to purchase. This was looked into and Eve decided that she wanted to buy a flat for herself. There were a great many difficulties for Eve initially in accessing her own money as she was under the Court of Protection (this will be further discussed in Chapter 5). However, these were overcome and Eve now lives in her own flat, assisted by a worker whom she refers to as *"my staff"* for 37.5 hours per week. The support worker gives Eve whatever help she feels she needs in order for her to live on her own. For Eve, her life has opened up tremendously to new experiences since moving out. She is in control of her own life:

> *"It's better to have your own house, you have more freedom to come and go."* (Eve)

She shops on a Monday, *"It's better then, there are not as many people there."* She predominantly cares for herself, does her own cooking and cleaning and so on. She is responsible for her own finances with assistance from her independent personal financial advisor. Eve has travelled widely and uses all of her local facilities. She visits her friends whenever she likes. She says that it took some time to get used to having her own freedom and living *"on the outside"*.

> *"It just took time I think, like things do... I think it is always hard when you make the change...I am glad I came out here."* (Eve)

Comments

As can be seen, the research participants live in a variety of settings managed by a variety of different service providers. The policy and strategic frameworks of the organisations, and how the individuals fit into the organisational structure, will be further discussed in Chapter 6. Good practice is relative to each area and the experiences of each individual. Living in the community is not sufficient on its own to guarantee a good quality of life as will be shown in the following chapter. The appropriateness of the various living environments, and what each individual considers to be good practice and how these practices develop, will be discussed further in the concluding chapter of this report.

3

What People Do With Their Time

"Most people with severe mental handicap have never worked in open employment, and unless they have received some form of regular day service, can look forward to an old age which is very similar to the rest of their lives." (Hogg et al. 1989)

Due to the age group of the research participants, daytime activity tended to be centred around recreation rather than any formal work-related occupation. However, there was a great variance in what people did with their time ranging from attending a segregated day service five days a week, to attending college, adult education, staying at home and going out to work. None of the participants was in full-time employment receiving an ordinary wage.

Daytime

For the people living in hospitals, formal daytime recreational facilities consisted of segregated clubs within the site. For Philip and Wilfred, there was a variety of clubs to attend during the day, though they were now part of the hospital 'over sixties club', and both attended this facility during the week. Wilfred also tended to spend quite some time wandering the extensive grounds of the hospital with a friend of his who lives on another ward. Within the ward in which Philip and Wilfred live, there were 'activity sessions' allocated through the day for those people who did not go to the day services. These included sessions on 'reality orientation' an interesting concept whereby events which are occurring outside in the 'real world' are discussed. However, for Wilfred this caused some confusion insofar as his understanding of what happens in the community is largely confined to news events which at times caused him distress:

> "Did you see the news about that man who killed all those people in Australia...all the time out there, people get killed." (Wilfred)

Events such as these troubled Wilfred and he said that he was safe where he was, "That doesn't happen here."

Both Philip and Wilfred rarely leave the hospital. Wilfred has an advocate, though he did not want to discuss her. He goes to her house now and again, and they go out into town together. As far as going out at any other time, according to Wilfred, *"I go into the community when it is my turn."* Philip spoke of a visit he made to Buckingham Palace:

> *"I was invited to attend, I'm in the 'not forgotten' club because I was a soldier."* (Philip)

For Edward and Terry, there is nothing at all to do all day long. As the rest of the hospital site is closed, there are not even any day facilities left for them to attend. Their days are spent *"lying on my bed, when they let me"* (Terry) or watching television on the ward. Edward goes to the sister hospital for treatment for his legs which is done on site, and occasionally the men go in the minibus to the shop there.

At Whales Hospital, day services were also provided on site, though there was evidence that there was a greater use of mobility cars to go out into town. Winnie went out on a couple of occasions after interviews, either to go shopping or into town.

Winnie, Arthur, Emily and Violet, when she was well enough, all attended the same club on site. In comparison to the clubs at the other hospital, this seemed to be far more organised towards the wishes of the individuals who attend. There was an area set aside for people to watch videos of old films containing news footage. This was popular amongst the people who attended, and they would talk about what they were watching and reminisce of days gone by. One of the facilitators at the club was enabling some of the people who attended to build a model railway based on a scaled down version of the local area. Winnie and Arthur spent their time chatting, cooking (Winnie gave me a cake recipe and told me how to make it) or doing whatever else took their interest that day.

Anne and her partner spent most of their time in one of the other clubs which, in the evenings, played host to the night entertainment:

> *"Me and my fella, we do our own thing. He's a fine fella, he's lovely. When I told him that there was a young woman asking after him he said, 'Well she can get lost, I've got a woman'."* (Anne)

Anne is accomplished at knitting and she considered this her work as she was always being asked to knit something for somebody:

> *"I make all these scarves and stuffed toys to order, if they want anything done they always come to me...I like to be busy, it's better to have something to do."*
> (Anne)

Maude, Maureen and Margery who live in the large housing association home, spend most of their time within the unit where they live. It is near to the local shops but few of the women are able to walk the distance and constraints on staff time dictate that this does not happen very often. They have craft mornings when a woman from the local day centre for people with learning difficulties comes in to knit and sew and chat with the women who live there. Maude is a very sociable person and has many stories to tell during these morning sessions. She often related a story of her past such as a time when she ran away from the institution where she was living and went to an orchard to pick apples:

> *"When I got back, they told me my passes and money would be stopped...I told them I don't care about the bloody money."*

Maureen and Margery spend much of their time together in their room, watching the television or chatting together. Maureen is very talented at needlepoint and has some of her work framed within the house. Margery spends her mornings in the kitchen assisting the cook in the preparation of lunch. All three of the women go to a cookery class in the town once a week and each attends a day centre in a local town when they want to. The house has a car which the women go out and about in quite often. Maude loves the seaside and spoke of *"eating chips in the back of the car...lovely"*.

Harry, Theresa, Tom, Henry and Connie who all live in housing association group homes, attend the same adult training centre. There are 131 people who attend the centre on a full or part time basis. The centre is located on the outskirts of town and is not within walking distance of the local facilities. It is a large building which has a hostel next door, though this is due to close. The centre offers a range of activities centred around groups of people. Activities such as arts and crafts, dance and working towards National Vocational Qualifications all occur at different times of the day. Theresa does not attend many of the structured activities, preferring to spend her time sitting in the foyer of the building *"just watching people*

26

go by" (Theresa). Theresa attends the local college two days a week in term time, as do Harry, Tom and Henry. Connie prefers not to attend college. The college offers courses in literacy and numeracy. Harry also spends a lot of time on his artwork at which he is particularly talented; an example of his work is shown at the front of this report. Tom has a job with a local firm of gardening contractors, which he does at weekends. Theresa works in a shop two days a week. Both Theresa and Tom place high value on the work that they do; both are volunteers and unpaid.

Jim and Mabel, who live in small group homes, Doris, who lives in a supported living network and Dorothy, who lives in sheltered accommodation, all attend the same day centre, though Jim only attends part time since his accident. The centre is due to close within the year and the day services will then focus on interest groups and the people attending will choose from a range of groups available. From the outside, the building which currently houses the day services looks abandoned and awaiting demolition. The outside door is kept locked at all times. The closure of the centre has upset some of those who attend. Mabel got her first ever job last year and she spends three days a week cleaning in a small office. She is very proud of this and talks as if she has been doing it for years!

Dorothy attends the centre every day and she spends most of her time there working in the kitchen helping the cook. She enjoys doing it and does not feel 'put upon'. She says that she likes the feeling of being useful - doing something valuable. The manager of the day centre says that: *"In effect, Dorothy works at the centre as an unpaid kitchen assistant."* They are trying to find money to pay her, but that can only be until the end of March when the centre closes. Dorothy refuses to consider what she will do after the centre does close.

Don, who lives in a small group home, goes out to work three days a week with a local carpentry firm, the other two days he spends at home. His work is very important to him:

> *"I don't want to retire, I want to stay at work."* (Don)

Don used to catch the bus to work though his health has recently deteriorated to the point where he now has to use dial-a-ride. As he has to pay for this, and as he does not get paid for his work, this is causing him some financial difficulties.

27

Gwen, who lives in the NHS Trust large community home, does not attend any formal day services and she spends most of her time at home. However, her advocate/friend Paul, spends time with her each week going swimming or to the cinema or whatever Gwen wants to do.

Fred, who lives in a warden-controlled bungalow, does not want to attend any day services and occupies himself looking after his home and his cats. He spends time with his neighbour, goes out shopping and potters around the garden. Generally, he does whatever he wants to do with his time.

Joseph, who lives in adult placement, has a job in a garage. This is important to him and earning £15 a week for what he does gives him a sense of achievement:

> *"I gets paid you know, I put it in the bank, I know how much money I've got, I'd like to get married so I'm saving up my money."* (Joseph)

He is very concerned that the garage where he works is relocating and he will be out of a job. He is adamant that he does not want to return to the day centre and is working with the employment officer from the day centre to try to find alternative employment.

Valerie, who lives with her brother, Bob, who lives in a residential home for older people, and Lily and John, who live in housing association small group homes, all attend a day centre which is specifically for older people with learning difficulties. This differs from the main day centre in that the pace is slower and less hectic. The centre is housed in what used to be the local primary school for the area. Activities on offer here tend to be based around the same craft-related pursuits as many other day services. People do not automatically have to attend the day centre for older people when they reach a certain age, but the option is open to them if they wish to do so:

> *"Ordinary ATCs are not always appropriate for older people."* (service manager)

However, it was noticeable that for much of the time people were sitting around the walls of one room doing very little. It was also apparent that people who attended the centre and the staff were sharply differentiated. The centre's manager, for example, explained why there are separate toilet facilities for the people who attend the centre and the people who work there:

"These people make a mess and I can't afford for my staff to be off sick because they've caught something from one of them." (day centre manager)

Respect and dignity are seemingly not an issue for this day centre. It would appear that a fundamental change in philosophy is required here.

This was the only example of a special day centre for older people with learning difficulties in the research.

Frank, who lives in the family home, attends a day centre which caters primarily for people with physical disabilities though he himself does not have a physical disability. He used to have a job in a local factory and was only meant to go to this particular facility as a temporary measure following a bout of ill health. However his keyworker at the centre felt it was a great mistake to have placed him there because:

"Even though it was meant to be temporary, he stayed here...you know how it is - once they come..." (Frank's keyworker)

Frank engages in light industrial work at the centre and occasionally he gets involved in other activities such as environmental studies, living skills and speaking up. According to his keyworker, his mother would not allow him to do anything 'dangerous', but since her death he has learned how to make things like tea, coffee and sandwiches. The only time he has ever been in a supermarket was when he went out with the living skills group.

"I like coming to the centre, I get bored at home." (Frank)

Eve, who lives in her own home, fills her day doing whatever she wants to do. She attends painting classes at her local college (they recently went away on a painting weekend): *"I've taken to using crayons now, it is much better than sploshing about with paint."* She used to attend an arts and crafts class as well until *"the teacher left for more money"*. She has learned to speak Spanish ready for the next time she goes on one of her many holidays, *"It's hard work that Spanish."*

29

Eve uses her local library and takes many day trips out, *"I went to visit Buckingham Palace but I couldn't live there it's too monumental."*

Eve cooks, cleans and maintains her home day-to-day, independently: *"He* (the manager of the organisation which provides her service) *wanted me to have someone two days a week but I didn't fancy it, I like to do it myself."* She runs her life the way she chooses to, visiting friends, taking walks - whatever she wants to do.

Evening

For the people in Heyton hospital, there was little in the way of evening recreation available other than watching the television or listening to the radio. Occasional evenings out to dinner were arranged on a rotational basis for Philip and Wilfred, though these were infrequent and were undertaken in groups.

For the people in Whales hospital, one of the clubs opened in the evenings serving alcohol if desired. There was entertainment laid on such as karaoke which Anne talked of with great enthusiasm:

> *"I love to sing the night away...I have three requests that they always ask me to sing."* (Anne)

For Maude, Maureen and Margery, there are occasional trips out in the evening or a choir comes in now and again to sing old-time music hall songs with the women. This was spoken of with much enthusiasm. The house is located next to a residential home for older people and when the house first opened some of the women were invited to attend a bingo evening with the elderly people next door. Unfortunately the women who attended had been used to the institutional way of playing bingo, where everybody wins all the time, and when this did not happen there was some disagreement between the people in the two houses. They were never invited again and the staff of the unit felt it best to leave things as they were.

For the people living in the small group homes, evening recreation is based on whatever each of them wants to do. Harry is very interested in the theatre. He has a season ticket and attends whatever performances he chooses. Others prefer to go to the pub with friends or to stay at home listening to music or watching the television.

Some of the participants were particularly isolated and prevented from attending any social events in their locality, either due to the nature of where they live or because the opportunities were not made available to them. Frank does not go out in the evening at all. He stays at home all the time and is never invited out with his family. As they are his only form of social contact when he is at home, he does not have any opportunity to go out with other people.

Eve goes out in the evening with friends or to her night classes though she prefers to be in after dark, *"I'm not too keen on being out at night."*

Holidays

For the people in Heyton hospital, holidays are organised on a group basis rather than around individuals' preferred destinations. The operational policy for the ward on which Wilfred and Philip live states that:

> *"Holidays and outings will be arranged for a group of 2-4 residents with individual choice and suitability."* (operational policy)

However, the ward newsletter stated that:

> *"8 residents went on holidays to* (a holiday camp) *for one week."*

For the people in Whales Hospital, holidays have been arranged in Europe as well as in the UK. However, it has been decided that each person being resettled should have a certain sum of money in their bank account when they move. For this reason, holidays are not a priority at the current time.

For the people in the group homes, each person has had a holiday this year to different destinations. Connie has been abroad with seventeen others on a trip run by the club she attends one evening a week. Harry was preparing for a holiday in an area where there is interesting architecture so that he could draw whilst he was there.

The majority of the people interviewed who had been on holiday had gone with a group of people. For those who did go alone it was to a segregated holiday hotel specialising in holidays for people with learning difficulties. For Don, in particular, using this facility meant that he could spend time on his own which is what he prefers to do. He travels alone to the hotel and has a break away from his carers and the people he lives with while at the same time receiving the support he requires. He does not have much money and could not afford to pay for a carer to accompany him on holiday.

Eve travels widely. She has many photograph albums crammed with pictures of her holidays. She has been all over Europe with one of her carers or with friends. She wanted to learn Spanish *"so that I might understand what they are going on about over there"*.

Comments

What people do with their time is dependent on where they live and who provides the service. For those living in hospitals, recreation and occupational facilities tend to be on site thereby further segregating the people who live there. However, those who do live in small group homes, or with relatives, also tend only to have access to segregated day facilities. There are organisational issues regarding age limits on the use of facilities and how this affects what is available to people. These issues will be discussed in Chapter 6. Good practice in this area is dependent on managers using foresight and creativity to provide person-centred services in the facilities that are available. There were examples of providers attempting to make the best use of the facilities on offer, such as in one area where the manager of the day service is pushing for closure of the existing service and working on developing a community-based resource rather than a building-based service.

Ways of achieving change will be discussed in the conclusions.

Finance is a major issue in this area. Organisational funding and personal wealth each play their part in determining what is available for the individual.

4

Networks

"It was clear that everyone could claim acquaintances but that friendship involving intimacy and reciprocity were much more rare." (Grant et al. 1995)

The length of this chapter highlights the fact that making and maintaining friendships is the largest area of deficit in the lives of people with learning difficulties.

Friendship is a difficult term to define; how we make friends and maintain them depends on our opportunities to go out and socialise with different groups of people. Access to ways of communicating with people is very important, such as writing letters, phone calls and the availability of transport to go out to social events. For people with learning difficulties this is often beyond their control. The environment within which people live is often one of care and duty rather than mutual enjoyment of each others company. If people only attend recreational and social facilities with the people they live with, or spend all day at day services with, the opportunity to meet new people is extremely limited:

"The biggest factor in quality of life, according to O'Brien's five principles, is that of making and having meaningful relationships. This was by far the biggest area of deficit in people's lives." (Walker et al. 1995)

Of the people interviewed for the research who lived in hospital, only one or two could cite meaningful relationships with people outside their living environment, which were not paid or arranged for them through an external agency such as an advocacy group. Philip has kept in contact with a friend he made many years ago and they still see each other now and again. His friend is getting older though and his health is deteriorating, so he is not able to visit Philip as much as he used to. Philip misses this relationship:

"I worry about him, he's not well you know. We used to go out into town for dinner but he can't drive anymore so I don't see him very often. We go back a long way." (Philip)

Philip does not go to visit his friend. He is not able to go on his own and nobody takes him.

Wilfred has an advocate whom he spends time with each week:

> *"I go to a house."* (Wilfred)

He fiercely protected his links with her and did not want to talk about her at all. He put great store on having something that was his alone, and which therefore seemed to give him a sense of value.

Due to the age of the research participants, few had relatives with whom they had contact. This was a cause of sadness to some:

> *"I'd like to see me sister more, but she lives miles away."* (Fred)

It hurts Winnie that some of the people she remembers from her past do not want to know her now:

> *"I don't think they know I'm in here."* (Winnie)

Nevertheless there was evidence of family links being maintained despite the distance and relative seclusion of the individuals' living environment:

> *"I've got the spare room at my niece's that I go to stay with once every month for the weekend."* (Anne)

Joseph lives with his partner in a flatlet within their carer's house. Tom would like to live with his partner but his relationship with her is restricted:

> *"I want to live with my girlfriend, but I only see her when she comes here* (to the centre) *her parents don't like it"* (Tom)

Family objections to relationships can present a very difficult obstacle at times. Joseph would like to have a more permanent, independent relationship with his partner but her family will not allow it:

> *"Why shouldn't we get married if that is what we want to do?"* (Joseph)

Intimate relationships between two people living in a residential home or other supported environment can lead to difficulties in administrative procedures, such as the need for the home to allow private, personal space and for the staff to have a supportive attitude towards the relationship. People living in supported environments are often perceived by staff to be 'better off' not engaging in intimate relationships. This tends to be typical of older persons' services generally. Older people, and in particular older people with learning difficulties, are often seen as not having the same sexual needs and desires as younger people. This notion sometimes leads to a lack of recognition of relationships as they develop:

> "He [a doctor] had also been urged by an agitated matron of an old people's home to commit a man to a psychiatric hospital because he had become engaged to a fellow resident. When the doctor refused to take such action the prospective bridegroom was moved to another home, twenty miles distant, and no contact, not even letters, was allowed between the couple. The prospective bride died a few weeks later." (Norman 1987)

However, current good practice guidance homes for older people encourages provision to be made for the maintenance of such relationships (CPA 1996).

Friendships can often begin in the place where people live, between themselves and their care workers. For older people this is less likely to be the case as carers are generally (due to retirement policy) younger than them and they may not have shared interests. The view that older people would prefer older carers, or links with people of a similar age, was echoed in the research:

> *"One of the carers who was working here when I first came was only 24 and she was working with 60 odd year olds...I thought she was a bit young...you don't want young ones looking after us old ones we've nothing in common, nothing to talk about."* (Eve)

The desire for sexual expression, sexual preferences and gender issues are important factors in defining where people should live, with whom and who should support them. There are some older people, particularly in institutional care, who have always lived with people of the same gender and do not wish to live in a mixed environment:

> *"I don't want to live in the same house as a woman, I can't share the same toilet can I?"* (Terry)

Mabel became quite uncomfortable when explaining that she shared a house with a man. She was keen to point out that the two of them do not have much to do with one another.

For older people generally, the loss of friends through bereavement or having to move to a different area leaves deficits in their social network that can be difficult to replace:

> *"A lot of people I used to know have died now... I'm 75 now, I'll not be twenty again."* (Eve)

Valerie lives with her brother who is 72 years of age. He worries about the time when he can no longer care for her and she will be forced to leave her home and the area she knows well.

> *"Who will look after her?"* (Valerie's brother)

Comments

The use of advocacy schemes has proven effective in widening the number of non-services people who interact with people with learning difficulties and older people generally (Dunning 1995). Paul has made a great difference in Gwen's life. However, advocacy is only a beginning in the development of a mutually fulfilling relationship. Widening people's experiences within their local community and the opportunity to pursue personal interests is an avenue which can open up new horizons for people. Eve, the woman who bought her own home, has made many friends in her local community by joining night classes and mixing with people who have mutual interests.

5

Choice and Control

"It is quite clear that the lives of mentally retarded people who live with their parents or residential care providers are overdetermined, one might say, because not only is their present day organised, arranged and regimented by other people, so is tomorrow and the future."
(Edgerton 1994)

The choice over where to live, what type of accommodation, locality, with whom and who to have as carers, is often restricted by organisational and policy issues. This chapter will concentrate on everyday choices which face each one of us and how the people in the research were enabled or encouraged to make those choices.

Flexibility

For the people living in hospital, everyday choices over basic issues such as what to eat and what time to get up, are dictated by the practices of the institution. Meals are served at regular times, the menu is set for each and every day. Within Heyton hospital there was no evidence of any flexibility in the regime at all. Meals are at set times, the evening meal being served at 4.15pm. The people who live there eat whatever is sent from the central kitchens. Drinks are served at a time decided by whomever is on duty at the time. For example, during an interview with Wilfred, I was offered a drink. Wilfred requested a drink and was told he had had one shortly before so he could not have another one. Neither Philip nor Wilfred have access to the kitchen and therefore have to rely on the staff making drinks for them. On one occasion during a visit to the ward, I was sitting at a table in the dining room with a cup of coffee. One of the men who lives on the ward asked if he could share it as he was thirsty. When I offered him the cup he said:

"Don't let the staff see me, it's one of their cups, not one of ours."

Yet during interviews with Terry and Edward, who live on a ward in the same hospital group, when I was offered a drink they were too. Such decisions seem to be arbitrary according to whomever is on duty at the time and perhaps the attitudes and philosophy of the ward manager.

At Whales hospital, although the main daily regime is similarly fixed, there was evidence of flexibility at times. For example during an interview with Anne, the ward manager asked if the people in the room at the time fancied what was for tea, when the reply was no he said he would make something different for them. Those who were able to had access to the kitchen to make a drink if they so wished.

The situation for those living in smaller residential group homes was markedly different insofar as the people were actively encouraged to devise menus, go shopping and make their own food and drink as required:

> "The cooking day-to-day is a shared activity, shared by staff and residents alike...all the everyday things are shared by the residents with staff helping out where necessary." (home manager)

Even in the large housing association group home which caters for nineteen older women, there is a fairly relaxed regime:

> "Breakfast is at anytime from when the first lady gets up until around 11.30am." (deputy home manager)

Facilities are available for the women to make drinks whenever they like without having to wait for a member of staff to do it for them.

There are naturally going to be organisational constraints which affect the lives of people living in groups, particularly large groups. However, a philosophy of care which recognises the individual as having the right to a choice made a big difference to the attitude of the care workers in each environment:

> "They have the freedom to come and go whenever they like from here. Each of them has a key to their own room and the front door." (home manager)

In contrast, within Heyton hospital, the ward manager spoke of the ward as being a place of work rather than the home of the people who live there. Improvements to the ward were expressed as making the ward a nicer place to work.

Respect

Respect for the individual as a person in his or her own right who deserves to be treated with dignity and respect was sadly lacking at times. Philip is an immensely proud man. He fought in the war, is always immaculately turned out and is extremely articulate and well spoken. He wears false teeth and during each interview his teeth were falling out as he did not have the correct fixative for them:

> *"I have asked for some of the powder to hold them in but they haven't got me any."* (Philip)

Edward also wears dentures, yet he only has a top set:

> *"They only gave me the top ones...the box said only top."*

When asked if he would like a bottom set he replied:

> *"Can't have them, they don't have them, only top."* (Edward)

In contrast, Winnie who lives in Whales hospital wears a wig. As soon as her wigs become untidy she goes out to buy more:

> *"I bought three new wigs today, do you like them, they are nice aren't they, I chose them."* (Winnie)

Eve, who lives on her own, makes all of her own decisions. She has support when she requires it and has access to independent advice for issues such as finance and home management.

Living in the family home does not necessarily afford individuals more choice and control over their lives. Frank does little for himself, he makes few decisions as his sisters do all this for him. He does not go shopping, choose what to eat or decide what to do with his time. He has as little control over his life as those living in hospital, perhaps even less.

Involvement in the Decision-Making Process

Individual programme plans are developed in meetings between the individual and all interested parties, such as those she or he spends time with, representatives of the environment she or he lives in and the day services, along with her or his advocate. They can be a way of encouraging individual choice and control over what people do with their time and what they would like to do. For some people this is effective. The people living in Whales hospital are all involved in the plans being made for resettlement. They have had a choice over where to go to live and with whom and are actively involved in orientation to their new environment.

For the people in Heyton hospital, the individual programme planning meeting (IPP) seems to be more for the organisation than for the individual. The principle of the individual programme plan is that it is formulated in accordance with the wishes and needs of the individual. The keyworker (the person who works most closely with the individual) should seek out the person's views before she/he seeks out those of other interested parties. However, in Heyton hospital:

> *"We usually do an assessment one or two months before IPP... we do it ourselves, not with him but with the other departments he goes to. The over sixties keyworker writes out his strengths and needs, and from our observation we write out his strengths and needs. I will write out all the strengths and needs on one piece of paper and then we discuss it at IPP meeting with Philip present."* (Philip's keyworker)

As Wynn-Jones (1994) states:

> "In such environments, being deprived of the dignity of making one's own decisions becomes the norm."

Finance

Money matters are closely linked to issues of choice and control. Whether individuals are in control of their money, and how it is spent, affects how much and to what extent they are able to influence many aspects of their lives (Bewley 1997).

Philip has a considerable amount of money which has been accrued through various means including benefits, ex-service pension and state pension. He lives on a ward which has recently been substantially renovated. A large conservatory has been built on the side of the ward. One of the members of staff informed me that Philip had paid for the conservatory. During one of our interviews, Philip confirmed this though he said that he does not go in there as people smoke in there and he does not like the smoke. Philip also said that he often signs the papers for money though he does not know what for.

Money is an issue which affects how much each individual can pursue their interests. Don used to use his bus pass to get to work, but now he has to pay for transport to get him there which leaves him with little money to use as he wishes.

Those who have control of their own money, collecting it from the post office and deciding, once the rent is paid, what to do with the rest, highly value this control:

> *"I collect my money, put some away and keep some for myself."* (Theresa)

It can cause frustration for those who do not have the opportunity to do this. Maureen used to go and collect her pension although she does not do this anymore and she does not know why:

> *"I used to go but then it just stopped, I don't know why."* (Maureen)

Eve, who now has total control over all her finances, was under the Court of Protection when she left the hospital. Eve's example is important in showing how people can get out of the control of the Court of Protection (for more detail on the difficulties encountered by individuals under the control of the Court of Protection see Bewley 1997). Being under their control caused Eve great difficulty and much frustration at times:

> *"They would come every year and ask lots of questions...I never looked after my own money...I couldn't just go shopping...I never saw a pension book, I just used to get a giro through the door."* (Eve)

Eve's GP was very helpful in assisting her to get out of the Court of Protection. She now has complete control of all her finances and uses the services of an independent financial advisor to assist her to manage her assets effectively.

Eve receives a war widow's pension. While she was under the Court of Protection, the national organisation of war widows lobbied for greater recognition of their needs and a national campaign was underway for some time. The Court of Protection did not inform Eve of any of this. She was not aware of what was happening and therefore could not take part or have her voice heard. She only became aware that there had been a campaign when it was all over. Now that she has complete control of her own finances, this is a situation which could not arise again.

Comments

The freedom to decide what to do with our money and our time is fundamental for most people. We all live within constraints of work or budgets but in essence, once we reach adulthood, we make our own decisions and live with the consequences. For people who do not have such choices, and maybe never have had, their lives are ruled by those in whose care they find themselves:

> "The sensation of being nobody can easily become the main experience of their years in 'protected' housing." (Lewis 1993)

As has been shown in this chapter, the philosophy of the carers, both personally and from an organisational perspective, can have a marked effect on the life of each individual.

6

Organisational Issues

"Older people and people with learning difficulties are individuals. Services must reflect that individuality and respond to individual needs. Stereotyping on the basis of age or disability is as unacceptable as doing so on the basis of race or gender."   (Walker et al. 1995)

None of the fieldwork areas had any specific policies or strategic plans for *older* people with learning difficulties. The organisational policies and strategic plans encompassed people with learning difficulties of all ages throughout the whole spectrum of need.

The Philosophy of Care

Respect for the needs and wishes of the individual varied between fieldwork areas quite markedly. This was not dependent on the size of the organisation or the number of people supported by it. In one area, in particular, the organisation's philosophy seemed to be guided by a very active parents' group whose philosophy drove the practices of the organisation. The hospital within this area has no closure plan in place as this is not what the parents' group wants: they want the hospital site to be developed into a village community. Whether this will happen will depend largely on whether or not the management of the hospital is prepared to implement national policy on closure and re-provision, or bow to pressure based on misunderstanding and fear of change. However, a senior member of the Trust felt that there was another agenda underpinning the lack of structured plans for closure:

> *"Personally I think there is a bit of an ambivalence about closing it. I think there is a business problem nowadays. In the past we didn't have these problems so you could follow your ideals. But now there is the Trust which has to keep the business going. There are far too many people who could lose a lot of money."*
> (senior member of the Trust)

Some of the workforce at Heyton hospital also played their part in encouraging the parents group to campaign against closure:

"I think that sometimes there is a collusion between the staff and parents to keep things as they are. There is a fair amount of subtle sabotage of discharges goes on." (senior member of the Trust)

This is in marked contrast to the ethos of the management at Whales hospital who have worked hard in stressing that the principal of resettlement is best for the individual and it is their needs which are paramount - not only the needs of the people living there but also those of all the workforce. There is an active policy to prevent redundancy, with the Trust pursuing individual choice for each member of staff. A policy document from Whales hospital, regarding the future employment of the staff, is the framework within which workers have been retrained into new areas of expertise or enabled to undertake further qualifications to make employment in the private sector a more viable option. For instance, all of the porters on site were offered the opportunity to gain HGV licences which would give them greater scope for employment when the hospital closes. Care staff have been offered courses to equip them with the necessary skills to work more effectively in community settings. The results of this have been that, in contrast to Heyton hospital, where the staff needs have been given a low priority and consequently staff do not support the closure plan for fear of losing their jobs, the staff in Whales hospital were, in general, far more receptive to the need for hospital closure. This was shown in the way they were more supportive of the individuals leaving the hospital.

Who Purchases/Provides the Services

The NHS and Community Care Act 1990 encouraged the use of joint commissioning of services between health and social services. The implementation of joint commissioning, as a procedure for the purchase of services, depends on the strategy of each authority. Which organisation is responsible for providing the funds depends on whether the individual requiring a service is defined as having predominantly health or predominantly social needs. This can cause some difficulty between the services and working relationships between health and social services can be strained by these difficulties:

"We could work more effectively with the health service, especially around older people. There is some duplication and confusion, though we are trying to sort that out. The (x) are doing a review of joint working and will come up with a plan to help us to work together." (social services manager)

The need to define whether a person has health or social needs in order to determine who will pay, often results in a service which does not look at the whole person and his or her overall needs, but one which focuses on specific needs which can be labelled and allocated to a service:

> *"There are perpetual arguments with the health authority about what it is that they are providing and what it is that we are providing, the continuing care arguments...by focusing on is it health is it social we are being chronically service-led. It is like saying this person needs a stairlift, this person needs a day service, do they heck, this person needs to get up and down stairs and this person needs to have something to do in the day time... Are they a health service or a social service, no they are a human being."* (social services manager)

For older people, whose needs may change with their increasing age, the situation becomes more complex in defining who will take responsibility for funding and provision of services. Social services often work, primarily, in teams: children, adult and older persons' services. When a person with a learning difficulty, who receives a service from the adult team's budget, reaches 65, the situation becomes even more blurred as to what will happen to them. The research found that whether they are transferred to the older person's team, or remain within the remit of the adult team, was dependent on area policy. However, none of the areas which participated in the research had a specific strategy to deal with this issue. The situation seemed to be dealt with through a series of unwritten agreements which suited both teams:

> *"The over 65s get funded through the elderly service in theory. In practice, some are and some aren't. What we're putting into practice now is that the learning difficulties teams will continue to care but funding will come from the elderly service."* (social services manager)

However, there is potential conflict where budgets are concerned as:

> *"Learning difficulties services are more expensive than elderly services, though so far it's been okay."* (social services manager)

Services for older people in general tend to be crisis-led and reactive rather than proactive. The number of people requiring services in relation to the funding which is allocated means that the service has to react to crisis situations rather than work towards preventing them. Most of the older people who are referred to social services departments and are assessed as needing services are very frail, often with dementia and require very high levels of support and care. This frequently means placement in residential or nursing home care, particularly if intensive packages of care to maintain them in their own homes are either inappropriate or too expensive.

In comparison, the services provided for people with learning difficulties, with their emphasis on small group home accommodation and provision of day services, are expensive. Hence the danger is that a person with a learning difficulty, who reaches the age of 65, may find their services cut dramatically from the level which they are used to. The nature of the social services interventions for older people tends to be one of crisis management, or targeting on the greatest need, rather than provision of regular support to people who are not in a situation of risk:

> *"It is only older people with extremely high support needs who get services."*
> (within the elderly team) (social services manager)

With regard to day service provision, the same age criterion is applied theoretically, though in practice it is not rigidly adhered to:

> *"We know within in-house day provision that there are people over 65 who are funded by the learning difficulties team. There has been no decision as to what should happen, we don't throw them out at 65."* (social services manager)

Eve left hospital with a package of care which provided for 37.5 hours per week support for her. At the time of writing this is adequate for her needs, but should she ever require more, she will be assessed as would other elderly people living in their own home and have to live with whatever decisions are made at that time. The future is uncertain for Eve in this respect. What will happen to her should she require greater support than she currently receives?

Registration

Many group homes are registered by the social services department under the Registered Homes Act 1984. A definition of the client group catered for has to be submitted with registration such as learning difficulties, mental health, elderly. An issue which arose in the research was what happens when a house is registered for people with learning difficulties and one of the people living there reaches 65? It seemed to depend on the particular organisation as to what the answer to that question might be. For some, it was merely a question of registering initially for both groups:

> *"We register for elderly, learning disability...even if not all of them are elderly, we have done this and been inspected and passed."* (homes manager)

For others it was considered that doing so would change the ethos of the home and therefore alternatives had to be sought:

> *"It would be a problem if they* (an elderly person with greater support needs) *wanted to stay...we are only very minimally staffed you see, so once people need more, if people come to the stage where they need more support, then they do need to go on to elderly care."* (home manager)

Registration officers have the power to grant a variance/discretionary statement to a home which is registered for learning difficulties and not elderly people if a person living there reaches 65 and the house is suitable to support their needs:

> *"It's monitored every year when the registration officer comes round. Somebody of Harry's age is actually vetted, for want of a better word, to see whether our support is enough to support somebody who may be having more added difficulties with the ageing process."* (home manager)

The need for registration and inspection of community homes is an issue which causes some difficulty amongst providers. The idea of living in an ordinary house, in an ordinary street forms the basis of what many people believe care in the community to be all about. However, there are elements of the registration requirements which are incompatible with this philosophy. One home manager described the difficulties like this:

> *"It's like jumping out of the frying pan and into the fire...with the institutions you could expect to have to have procedures for every eventuality.... But the idea of community living is to provide ordinary housing and to live in the same way as our neighbours, yet we have to have fire extinguishers on display, fire exit signs on doors and so on... I don't have them in my home...we also have to have*

a visitors book which anyone coming in must sign. Is that ordinary living?"
(home manager)

The Decision-Making Process

How much each person is involved in decisions regarding the allocation of resources for their support was dependent on the area within which they lived. Service planning issues were dealt with primarily by management with little or no user involvement at all:

> *"We don't have an effective way of involving users in joint planning. We have a joint planning process that users are not involved in at all. We are trying to do something about that too."* (social services manager)

For one of the areas, the allocation of resources was tightly tied to the assessment of risk for each individual:

> *"I am actually really having to target on risk and I am having to look at those people who are really in dire straits"* (social services manager)

The outcome of this policy for the individual is that a service will only be provided if the person is assessed as being in the highest category of risk. The danger here is that an older person living at home with an older relative and with little service input may not be considered at immediate risk. Therefore, there is no strategy in place should there come a time when the carer dies or can no longer care adequately for their relative. The result is that a crisis will almost inevitably happen, and the individual may find themselves in a situation where they are forced away from everything that they know and into a service which is not geared to their needs. This is the situation for older people in general and one which services for people with learning difficulties must seek to avoid.

Other areas are looking at ways of overcoming this potential crisis situation in various ways:

> *"We are not unhappy for the ailing parent to move into a residential home with the son or daughter with a learning disability, it leaves the options open after the parent's death."* (social services manager)

Another area stated:

> *"We need to become proactive rather than reactive...we should have some kind of a rapid response team for a crisis who can drop everything and manage a situation until the best solution can be found."* (social services manager)

Comments

The lack of specific policies for older people with learning difficulties leaves the field open for services to define how they provide for each individual. In many respects this is a positive aspect insofar as it allows for flexibility to provide a more person centred service. However, there are difficulties which mean that people with learning difficulties reaching 65 often find themselves in a situation where nobody seems to have overall responsibility to assess and meet their needs, and they have to fit into whatever is available at the time. According to the service providers, age in itself does not seem to be the determining factor. It seems that how increasing age has affected the individual, such as whether their mobility has decreased, is more likely to influence where they fit into service provision.

The concluding chapter will consider whether or not specific policies would be advantageous in the long term for older people with learning difficulties.

7

Conclusions and Recommendations

This chapter brings together the points raised in the report and highlights examples of good practice. It identifies areas where services are working in the right direction and ways of achieving better practice within existing frameworks.

Where People Live

The research looked at services available to older people with learning difficulties within two NHS Trusts and three local authority social service departments. There were marked differences between the philosophy and practices of the two NHS Trust hospitals. Government policy states that people with learning difficulties should be enabled to live within the community. Of the three hospital sites visited during the fieldwork, only one is actively pursuing this policy. Whales hospital has a clear strategy for resettlement of all the people living there with the end objective of closing the hospital. For the people living in Heyton hospital, it is an ad hoc process and there is no clear strategy at all for the future of the site. There is not, therefore, a clear objective to resettle older people with learning difficulties at Heyton hospital.

Similarly, within the local authorities there were differences in philosophy and practice, though on a lesser scale as many of the people interviewed live in similar environments. The main differences were how the philosophy of the service managers affected delivery of services and what their aims for the future development of community care were. For some areas, the lack of policy aims on closure and resettlement did not inhibit their practice. The fundamental difference was one of attitude towards the individuals and providing a better life with greater opportunities in the most appropriate setting for each individual.

Recommendations

- all hospitals should look at the best examples of good practice available. There are opportunities to learn from hospitals which are in the process of successful resettlement and closure, and greater information sharing should be encouraged;

- the impetus for resettlement should not be expected to come from the people living in hospital. When people have lived in the same environment for many years with little experience of alternative living environments, it is unlikely that they will request change. There needs to be more information given to individuals about alternatives and the opportunity to discuss alternatives should be part of the operational policy for each ward;

- there needs to be clear policy direction from national government, to ensure that good practice guidance is consistently followed. This needs to include a clear objective to resettle older people with learning difficulties as well as younger people;

- people with learning difficulties have as much need, when they grow old, for opportunities to make friends and engage in fruitful social relationships and activities as other older people do. Service providers must recognise this and respond to these needs.

Philosophy

The research involved people living in a variety of different environments. It was clear that the philosophy operating within each made a marked difference to the practice of the staff. Direct care workers learn from the philosophy and practice of the organisation for which they work. If the philosophy is one of promoting independence and inclusion in the decision-making process then good practice is more likely to be the result. Many of the housing associations followed a philosophy of inclusion and promoting independence, and the research found that the people living within them had more opportunities to experience ordinary living and to take more control of their own lives.

Recommendations

- service managers need to provide direct care staff with a clear philosophy of care based on good practice;

- all those affected by decisions taken should be involved in the decision-making process at all levels. At a senior level this can be achieved by the use of independent advocates, where necessary, to represent the needs and wishes of the people who live there and by appointing representatives of the staff team to put across the views of the staff. On a day-to-day level, each individual must play an active part in the individual programme planning process, either in person or through an advocate;

- staff also have to be considered when planning the closure of a hospital. If the staff feel they have everything to lose and nothing to gain, then their co-operation and support of the process is less likely to be forthcoming. Whales hospital devised an positive process whereby staff were offered retraining in new skills to enable them to have a greater chance of employment when the hospital closed. This had a marked effect on the amount of co-operation and support which was offered to the people being resettled and on maintaining higher standards in practice during the run-down of the hospital. Other hospitals should consider instigating a similar process to prevent the *"subtle sabotage of discharges"*.

A Place of Work or a Person's Home?

The research found evidence that some of the settings where people lived were regarded primarily as places of work rather than as people's homes. The philosophy of the organisation providing the service influences the way the environment where people live is viewed. In hospital, there is often a profound failure to recognise the ward primarily as a place where people live. Comments in a ward newsletter, for example, which referred to the new decor as making it a nicer place to work, are not untypical.

Even though it may be a remote hospital ward, it is home to all of the people who live there. Having inaccessible rooms, not because of restricted physical access but because they are staff areas, adds to the perception that people living there are incidental to the reality that it is a place of work. Having separate cups for those who work there is degrading and dehumanising for the people who live there.

The people living in housing association group homes had far greater access to the whole house. Many had keys to their own rooms and front door keys with the freedom to come and go as they pleased.

Registration of a group home can add to the impression that it is a place of work before being somebody's home. The need for fire exit signs on doors, fire extinguishers, hygiene requirements in the kitchen and so on, help to create a sterile, institutional air in what should be an ordinary house. This is a dilemma for organisations as greater regulation is often assumed to be a means of raising standards. The possible conflict between the consequences of regulation and other safety legislation on the home environment, and the aim to create 'real homes' in 'real communities', is one which many organisations face.

Recommendations

- that each organisation has a clear philosophy that the environment where people live is primarily their home and that practice must reflect this;

- that registration and inspection procedures place more emphasis on the quality of care practice within the home, ensuring that the physical environment is conducive to people's emotional as well as physical well-being.

Care Management

The care manager is most usually the person responsible for assisting individuals to move on from where they live. To find a suitable place to live, based solely on current needs, may not provide the best solution for an older person. For example, as noted earlier in the report Jim, who lives in a housing association group home, moved in when he was in his late fifties. The environment suited him at that time, he was quite able to manage stairs and care for himself independently. However, he had an accident which has left him with reduced mobility and a need for greater assistance with daily living skills. Had his care manager worked with him in looking beyond the first few years of his placement, his accident may not have caused him to be so restricted in his own home.

Jim and his carers are now unsure of what will happen to him should his mobility not improve sufficiently for him to remain where he is with the resources available. This is causing some concern to Jim and his carers as they do not know how to move forward and enable him to make plans for his future. Jim's example illustrates the longer term perspective which must be taken when older people are being resettled or are moving house.

Recommendations

• when an older person is going through the process of resettlement or moving into a residential facility of any kind, care managers need to think about what needs the individual may have in 10-15 years time. Thus, if people of 60 are moving on from where they live, care managers should assist them in seeking out a place to live which will be able to support them should their needs increase with age. This does not mean that a person needs to move into an environment which will stifle independence or lead to a loss of skills through dependency. But it does mean that if a person's physical needs change or increase, then the living environment and social support should be able to adapt accordingly. This might be achieved by creating downstairs bedrooms or otherwise adapting the house to meet changing needs. This would be more feasible if it was acknowledged in the original care plan for the individual;

• the care manager should maintain a presence within the person's life so that situations such as Jim's can be effectively managed as soon as difficulties arise. For older people generally, changes in health needs may require effective intervention at an early stage and care managers can play a useful role in monitoring any changes with the direct care team;

• effective communication and information exchange should be co-ordinated by the care manager. Information exchange is a crucial factor in ensuring that all relevant parties are aware of the situation and the possible options. Opportunities should be made for all involved to discuss the issues.

Who Is Responsible?

The research found that in some social services departments the responsibility for providing and funding services for older people with learning difficulties is shared between the older persons and adults teams, and that sharing is based on unwritten agreements between the teams. These unwritten agreements give a degree of flexibility in provision, which facilitates the provision of the desired support. However, the resources available to the older persons team are limited. Support for people with learning difficulties tends to reflect ordinary life principles more often than the support available to people in older people's services. Older people who have a learning difficulty may, therefore, lose out if the resources available to the older persons team are stretched too thin. But this raises questions about the resourcing of older people's services more generally. These services, too, should be better resourced.

Recommendations

- that social service teams begin a consultation process aimed at clarifying the responsibilities each of them has towards older people with learning difficulties;

- that the benefits to the older person with a learning difficulty of having access to a variety of skills are not lost in this process.

What People Do With Their Time

The research found that segregated day services were the only option available to the majority of older people with learning difficulties. None of the participants in the research who used the day services attended any form of integrated day facility. Some people did attend courses at local colleges, but they did not attend older persons' clubs or societies in the wider community. There are many and varied clubs which are available to older people, such as lunch clubs or Age Concern day centres. During interviews, many people expressed the desire to be part of a group whose interests were similar to their own, such as reading, watching old films, singing songs from old films and musicals. These interests are shared by many older people and this could be a prime focus for fuller integration. Such integration could lead to the building of new social networks for people who have previously been confined to socialising on a very narrow level. However, integration will not necessarily happen easily, as those who have been used to a particular way of doing things will not always find it easy to adapt to a different way. For instance, the example from the research of the women who went to join their neighbours for a bingo session and were not invited back. Such steps towards integration need to be carefully planned and implemented if they are to be successful.

Recommendations

- within existing day service provision for people with learning difficulties, there is scope for much improvement. Setting aside areas where older people with learning difficulties can sit and read quietly or listen to music, watch films and so on, is something which is achievable now;

- setting up separate day centres for older people with learning difficulties, although it offers something different from the regular day centres for people with learning difficulties, is not the way forward. Instead of making a separate resource, the staff team at the centre could be working towards including the older people in the services which already exist for older people in general;

- service managers should focus on moving people out of segregated services and into ordinary community facilities;

- holidays and outings could be an opportunity for people to experience alternative living environments. Group holidays to camps or segregated hotels do not allow for such experiences to occur. Individuals should be encouraged to pursue their own interests rather than joining group activities which have no relevance to them, as in the example of Wilfred. Learning from the example of Harry, who went on holiday to an area where there were buildings of architectural interest that he could draw, can be particularly valuable.

Funding

How the health and local authorities work together to make the best use of available resources is an important factor in determining whether or not individuals get the best possible service. Competing budgets and inter-agency definitions of who should provide for whom, can work to the detriment of the individual. The health and social services need to work together to maximise resources rather than seek to define whether a person has primarily health or social needs.

The closure of the hospitals releases revenue that can give a person moving out a better start. In the case of Whales hospital, for example, it was *"...felt that not only should individuals leaving the institution come with a dowry which is part of the revenue...but would carry a piece of the capital as well, the actual resource..."* (regional officer). This resulted in the fact that *"three or four people could actually purchase a property and have it permanently for their life or as long as they needed it"* (regional officer). This is a positive step towards acknowledging that people who have lived in one place for a long time have a financial interest in it. It gives individuals a chance to purchase an interest in the property they are moving into which itself gives greater security in terms of tenure.

Recommendations

- the services need to find ways of working together in order to provide a cohesive, person-centred service;

- there should be greater information exchanges between districts in order to pass on effective ways each has found of using the resources available.

Personal Money

The research found that the amount of control each person had over their own money was often determined by the organisation and not by the individual. People living in group homes tended to have greater control over their own money than those in hospital and were actively encouraged to look after it themselves. Enabling a person to go to the bank or building society and collect or deposit their own money is a very empowering exercise. Some of the older people interviewed for the research had substantial sums of money accrued through pensions as well as benefits. Money, and the lack of control over it, was an issue which caused great distress to some of the people interviewed: from not knowing why they could not collect it from the post office themselves, to not knowing why certain items were purchased for them or even how much money they had.

This was highlighted most profoundly by the contrasting positions of Eve and Philip. Eve wanted to move on from where she lived. The people who supported her were keen to find out what she wanted and so began the process of her buying her own home. The fact that her support workers were prepared to look beyond the obvious, beyond her moving into another shared, rented flat or house, led the way to Eve living her life the way she wants to, enabling her to use her money and her support workers in ways that many people with learning difficulties could not even imagine.

Philip, on the other hand, who was a soldier in World War II and gained medals for his bravery, lives in a hospital ward which is completely segregated from the wider community. His money has been used to purchase items such as a television he does not watch and a conservatory he does not use. He was not asked what he would like to spend his money on, he was simply given a money order to sign. Philip has enough money to buy his own home, or to pay for the items, trips and support that would give him pleasure. As a soldier he travelled the world, yet he has never been abroad on holiday from the hospital. He has a friend who lives some distance away who is ill, but he has never been supported to visit him.

Some of the people interviewed had made a will. However, this seemed to depend on where they lived and was not standard practice in any of the areas. It is a positive move to enable people to stipulate what they want to happen to their assets when they die, but the process does need to be thoroughly explained. Philip has made a will but he was under the impression that he could no longer spend his money, as he had promised it to somebody else.

Philip's life could be opened up to a whole new dimension, as Eve's has been, if only there were somebody supporting him who was willing to listen to him. Eve's money has worked for her in giving her so many opportunities; Philip's money has simply made him an asset to the ward.

Recommendations

- each individual needs to have more control over his or her own money. This can be done by enabling people to become more involved with collecting and depositing their own money in a bank, and by supporting people to think through what they would like to do with their money (for more information on money control see Bewley 1997);

- older people who have amassed money in banks and building societies should be encouraged to talk about how they would like to spend it;

- older people should have the opportunity to make a will if they so wish, but the process must be clearly explained in detail to avoid misunderstandings.

Appendix 1: The research participants and where they live

Type of accommodation	Name	Age	Total residents
NHS Trust Hospitals			
Seal Hospital	Terry	67	10 on ward
	Edward	81	
Heyton Hospital	Wilfred	77	19 on ward
	Philip	84	
Whales Hospital	Arthur	70s	
	Winnie	70s	
	Anne	81	
	Emily	70	
	Violet	86	
NHS Trust Large Community Home	Gwen	60s	16
Housing Association Large Home	Maureen	84	19
	Maude	80	
	Margery	79	
Housing Association Small Group Homes			
Calder	Jim	66	4
	Don	60s	
Allons	Theresa	58	5
	Tom	56	
Kielder	Harry	61	7
Brant	Mabel	62	2
Buttermere	John	70s	6
	Lily	70s	6
NHS Trust Small Community Home	Henry	61	3
Housing Network Scheme	Doris	59	

Type of accommodation	Name	Age	Total residents
Adult Placement Scheme	Connie	64	3+ carer
	Joseph	60	2+carer
Residential Home	Bob	70s	38
Sheltered Housing/Warden Control	Dorothy	59	
	Fred	68	
Living with Relatives	Frank	57	
	Valerie	68	
Own Home	Eve	75	

References

Arber, S. and Ginn, J. (1995) (Eds) *Connecting Gender and Ageing: a sociological approach*, Open University Press: Buckingham.

Bewley, C. (1997) *Money Matters: helping people with learning difficulties have more control over their money*, Values Into Action: London.

Blewett, T. (1980) 'The Search for Identity in a Residential Home for the Elderly', *Social Work Today* 11(22), 5 February.

Bytheway, W. (1995) *Ageism*, Open University Press: Buckingham.

Centre for Policy on Ageing (1984) *Home Life: a code of practice for residential care*, Centre for Policy on Ageing: London.

Centre for Policy on Ageing (1996) *A Better Home Life: a code of good practice for residential and nursing home care*, Centre for Policy on Ageing: London.

Collins, J. (1992) *When the Eagles Fly: a report on the resettlement of people with learning difficulties from long-stay institutions*, Values Into Action: London.

Collins, J. (1993) *The Resettlement Game: policy and procrastination in the closure of mental handicap hospitals*, Values Into Action: London.

Collins, J. (1994) *Still to be Settled: strategies for the resettlement of people from mental handicap hospitals*, Values Into Action: London.

Dunning, A. (1995) *Citizen Advocacy with Older People: a code of good practice.* Centre for Policy on Ageing: London.

Edgerton, R.B. (1989) 'Ageing in the Community: a matter of choice', in Brechin, A. and Walmsley, J. (Eds), *Making Connections*, Hodder and Stoughton in Association with the Open University: London.

Edgerton, R.B. (1994) 'Quality of Life Issues: some people know how to be old', in Mailick Seltzer, M., Wyngaarden Krauss, M. and Janicki, M.P. (Eds) *Life Course Perspectives on Adulthood and Old Age*, American Association on Mental Retardation: Washington DC.

Godlove, C., Richard, L. and Rodwell, G. (1982) *Time for Action: an observation study of elderly people in four different care environments*, University of Sheffield Joint Unit for Social Services Research: Sheffield.

Grant, G., McGrath, M. and Ramcharan, P. (1995), 'Community Inclusion of Older People with Learning Disabilities', *Care in Place* 2 (1), March.

Heller, T. (1985) 'Residential Relocation and Reactions of Mentally Retarded Persons', in Janicki, M.P. and Wisniewski H.M. *Ageing and Developmental Disabilities: issues and trends,* Paul Brookes: Baltimore.

Hogg, J., Moss, S. and Cooke, D. (1989) 'From Mid-Life to Old-Age: ageing and the nature of specific life-transitions of people with mental handicap', in Horobin, G. and May, D. (Eds) *Living with Mental Handicap: transitions in the lives of people with mental handicap,* Jessica Kingsley Publishers: London.

Lewis, M. (1993) 'Some Thoughts on Visits to Old People's Homes', in *Elders: the Journal of Care and Practice* 2(3), August.

Midwinter, E. (1992) *Citizenship: from ageism to participation.* The Carnegie Inquiry into the Third Age. Research Paper Number 8. Carnegie UK Trust and Centre for Policy on Ageing: London.

Norman, A. (1987) *Aspects of Ageism: a discussion paper,* Centre for Policy on Ageing: London.

SSI (1997) Services for Older People With Learning Disability - Report of a Social Services Inspectorate, July 1997.

Stocker, B., Ethrington, A. and Whittaker, A. (1995) *Moving From Hospital into the Community: an evaluation by people with learning difficulties,* Joseph Rowntree Foundation Findings, Social Care Research 64, March.

Walker, C., Walker, A. and Ryan, T. (1993) *Quality of Life After Resettlement for People with Learning Disabilities.* Report to the North West Regional Health Authority, January.

Walker, C., Walker, A. and Ryan, T. (1995) 'What Kind of Future? Opportunities for Older People with a Learning Difficulty', in Philpot, T. and Ward, L. (Eds) *Values and Visions: changing ideas in services for people with learning difficulties,* Butterworth and Heinemann: Oxford.

Walker, C., Walker, A. and Ryan, T. (1996a) *Fair Shares For All?,* Pavilion Publishing: London.

Walker, A., Walker, C. and Ryan, T. (1996b) 'Older People with Learning Difficulties Leaving Institutional Care - A Case of Double Jeopardy', *Ageing and Society* 16, pp. 125-150.

Wynn-Jones, A. (1994) 'The Elderly Person with Mental Handicap', *Mental Handicap* 12, March.

Further Reading

Barr, O. and Fay, M. (1993) 34 'Community Homes: institutions in waiting?', *Nursing Standard* 7(41), June 30.

Felce, D., Beyer, S. and Todd, S. (1995) 'A Strategy for All Seasons', *Community Care*, 3-9 August.

Fennell, G., Phillipson, C. and Evers, H. (1988) *The Social Theory of Old Age*, Open University Press: Buckingham.

Hatton, C. and Emerson, E. (1984) 'Moving Out', *The Health Service Journal*, 19 May.

Hogg, J., Moss, S. and Cooke, D. (1988) *Ageing and Mental Handicap*, Croom Helm: London.

Hudson, B. (1990) 'Ignored But Still Needed', *The Health Service Journal*, 1 March.

Hulbert, R.J. and Lens, W. (1988) 'Time and Self Identity in Later Life', *International Journal on Ageing and Human Development* 27(4).

O'Brien, J. (1987) *A Guide to Personal Futures Planning*, Responsive Systems Associates: Atlanta.

O'Brien, J. and Lyle, C. (1989) *Framework for Accomplishments*, Responsive Systems Associates: Atlanta.

Powell, R. (1996) 'A Fresh Start', *Community Care*, 4 July.

Russell, O. (1994) 'Sister Act', *Community Care*, 27 January.

McGowan, C. (1996) 'A Long Way from Home', *The Health Service Journal*, 25 April.

Nicholson, N. and Paley, J. (1981) 'What Are the Principles of Practice?', *Community Care*, 30 July.

Norman, A. (1982) *Mental Illness in Old Age: meeting the challenge*, Centre for Policy on Ageing: London.

Simons, K. (1995) *My Home, My Life*, Values Into Action: London.

Thompson, P. (1995) *Age and Dignity: working with older people*, Arena: Aldershot.

Walker, C., Walker, A. and Ryan, T. (1995) 'A Step in the Right Direction: people with learning difficulties moving into the community', *Health and Social Care in the Community* 3(4), pp. 249-259.

Walker, C., Walker, A. and Ryan, T. (1995) *Disparities in Service Provision for People with Learning Difficulties Living in the Community.* Joseph Rowntree Foundation Findings, Social Care Research 75, December.

Walker, C. (1996) 'Levelling the Odds', *Community Care,* 23-29 May.

Weinberg, J.K. (1987) 'Ageing and Dependence: toward a redefinition of autonomy', *Social Casework: The Journal of Contemporary Social Work* 68(9), November.